Text © 2021 June Cotner and Nancy Tupper Ling • Illustrations © 2021 Helen Cann

Published in 2021 by Eerdmans Books for Young Readers, an imprint of Wm. B. Eerdmans Publishing Co., Grand Rapids, Michigan
www.eerdmans.com/youngreaders • All rights reserved • Manufactured in China

29 28 27 26 25 24 23 22 21   1 2 3 4 5 6 7 8 9

ISBN 978-0-8028-5519-0

A catalog record of this book is available from the Library of Congress.

Illustrations created with watercolor, collage, and colored pencil

FOR EVERY LITTLE THING

POEMS AND PRAYERS
TO CELEBRATE THE DAY

POEMS SELECTED BY
JUNE COTNER & NANCY TUPPER LING

ILLUSTRATED BY
HELEN CANN

EERDMANS BOOKS FOR YOUNG READERS

GRAND RAPIDS, MICHIGAN

For my four grandchildren—
Shay, Weston, Kailen, and Camille.

— J. C.

With gratitude to June, Anne Marie,
Gordon, and Joan—my movers and shakers.
Soli Deo Gloria.

— N. T. L.

For Esther, Tom, Martha, Benjamin,
and Eden Sweeney,
with much love.

— H. C.

TABLE OF CONTENTS

A NOTE ABOUT THIS BOOK

When a child expresses gratitude, the world feels like a better place. What a delight it is when children notice the sunlight falling upon their comforter or the sweet, sloppy kiss from their puppy. Surely, a child with a thankful heart makes us smile. Often this sense of appreciation comes from observation, and while it can be spontaneous and natural, it can also be a practice that we help instill in our children.

Our hope is that families will celebrate the wonders of the universe as they read together. *For Every Little Thing* will take a child from morning to night with easy-to-read, memorable selections that families will treasure. Each prayer, poem, and blessing offers an appreciation for the small and big gifts of the world. Here, children can discover thankful hearts for their daily blessings and a personal way to draw closer to God and one another.

These snippets of joy and wisdom are told through a variety of voices, many of them award-winning poets. Selections include verses by Christina Rossetti and Emily Dickinson and modern reflections from Rabbi Rami M. Shapiro and Arlene Gay Levine. The book can be read anytime during the day, but it will be especially appreciated as a bedtime book in which a parent and child can talk about the day through the lens of gratitude. We envision a child turning to their favorite section, whether it's "Family and Friends" or "Dreams," to find words of gratitude that become a familiar comfort to them. Perhaps we will all begin to stop in our tracks to admire a caterpillar or offer a new grace at mealtime. Truly our hope is that these words will help grown-ups and children celebrate their day in a whole new way.

With gratitude,

June and Nancy

FOR EVERY LITTLE THING

For morning song and gentle brook,
a faithful friend, a favorite book,
for robin's eggs and swinging trees,
the daffodils and dancing bees—

For lady bugs and butterflies,
bluebirds, breezes, cloud-filled skies,
for kitten's mew and horse's neigh,
the golden sun that ends my day,

I thank my God for scales and wings,
for each and every little thing.

— Nancy Tupper Ling

Morning

MY DAY BEGINS WITH KISSES

My day begins with kisses,
the slobbery, doggy kind.
That's how my puppy wakes me up,
I guess I shouldn't mind.

I know he wants his breakfast;
he's waiting to be fed.
I simply wish he wouldn't drool
across my sleepy head.

— Susanne Wiggins Bunch

WAKING UP PRAYER

I like to wake up when the sun is bouncing
like a yellow beach ball
against my bedroom wall.

I like to wake up when the rain is parachuting
from the sky
and landing on my roof.

I like to wake up and hear the wind chase
its tail, fast then slow,
racing off with a whoosh and a whistle.

I like to wake up when the snow falls
against my window
like confetti from an angel's party.

I like to wake up and find
the surprise
God has made for me today.

— Susan J. Erickson

MORNING

Open my eyes,
what do I see?
More loving eyes,
smiling at me.
I jump out of bed
into puddles of light—
arms outstretched
to hug me tight.

— Annie Dougherty

SEEING YOU

Dear God,
When I open my eyes this morning
please let me see You.
You on the bus;
You in my teachers;
You in my friends;
You in those that love me;
You in those that scare me;
You in what makes me happy;
You in what makes me sad;
You in all the places I expect;
You in all the places I don't.

— Rabbi Rami M. Shapiro

THE WONDERER

The sun is up
and so am I
to wonder
at the morning sky.

The shifting clouds
the birds on wing
the cooling air
that fresh rains bring.

I feel the wind
I touch the earth
I celebrate
a new day's birth.

I too am part
of all I see
for my dear God
gives life to *me*!

— Daniel Roselle

I'LL TELL YOU HOW THE SUN ROSE

I'll tell you how the sun rose, —
    A ribbon at a time.
The steeples swam in amethyst,
The news like squirrels ran.

The hills untied their bonnets,
The bobolinks begun.
Then I said softly to myself,
"That must have been the sun!"

— Emily Dickinson

CREATION

Today I saw the sun come up
and everything was hushed.
To me it seemed pure magic
to watch the world appear
as piece by piece it fell in place
all painted by Your brush.

— Arlene Gay Levine

YOU'RE EVERYWHERE . . .

In the wings of morning,
the sand on the beach.
Let me hear You in the birds
and the bumblebees.
Hug me with limbs of trees.
Bump into me, God.
Everywhere.

— Marion Schoeberlein

REJOICING

Everything is glad today
in a squeaking, piping, twittering way
all earth's creatures are having their say
with winging, singing, whispery sounds
with purring, barking, and racing around.

— Patricia Spears Bigelow

MY BEAUTIFUL DAY

I borrowed a poem from the sky,
and music from a bird,
I stole a chime out of the wind,
and from the rose a word,
I borrowed a song from the hills,
a psalm from the silver rain,
I took the footsteps of angels
out of a cobbled lane,
from each little thing I fashioned
something in my own way,
with God's help I put in my heart
a wonderful, beautiful day!

— Marion Schoeberlein

The World Around Us

WHEREVER I AM

Wherever I am
God is . . .

On the sand by the sea,
in a forest by a tree.

In the quiet of the night,
through the darkness,
in the light . . .

In the rain—in the cold,
in the wind blowing bold!

Through the chill in the air,
in my joy, everywhere . . .

Wherever I am
God is . . . with me.

— Fanny M. Levin

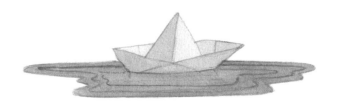

THE FIREFLIES ARE BACK!

A glitter of light on a warm June night.
    The fireflies are back!
A neon display, spelling out "Hurray!
    The fireflies are back!"
Golden-tailed kings! Fireworks with wings!
    The fireflies are back!
Make a wish on a star in a Mason jar.
    The fireflies are back!

— Bill McTaggart

BUGS

Big bugs under leaves
going places nobody sees

— Nicole VanderMeer, age 8

THE BEACH

Come walk with me,
barefoot in sand beside the sea,
where white gulls squawk
and sandpipers run.

Curl your toes in the water,
wave at the boats,
build castles with moats,
collect tiny shells,
all colors and kinds,
arrange them in sand
till they spell out your name
in circles and lines.

When light leaves the sky
and birds go to sleep,
when the water is still
and the boats have gone home,
pick up your shells
and say "thank you" for play,
for the beach, for the sun,
for the fun of this day.

— Jane Mary Curran

I believe that God is in me
as the sun is in the color and the fragrance
of a flower—
the Light in my darkness,
the Voice in my silence.

— Helen Keller

Everything in nature is a wonderful miracle!
Isn't the little bird flying through the big sky a miracle?

— Amma

THE BUTTERFLY BALLET

Dancing over the garden
in their orange shoes,
laughing on the grasses,
playing on the dews,
stealing sunbeam kisses,
running in the rain,
flying black-jeweled flowers
in a country lane,
colors of the rainbow
in your pretty wings,
ballet of the butterflies
as the summer sings.

— Marion Schoeberlein

SKY DANCERS

They loop, they spin, they pirouette
while dancing in the sky.
They glide, they dip, they do-si-do,
then gently rest nearby.

Their costuming so intricate,
so fine in each detail,
reveals a heavenly artistry
which is, each spring, unveiled.

Their performances are seasonal.
Their shows are always free.
New dancers will emerge each day
to dance for you and me.

For each dance they are rewarded
with a colorful bouquet.
They gently sip its nectar and
then butterfly away.

— Susanne Wiggins Bunch

SOMETIMES

Sometimes I wish
I could soar on high;
reach around and touch the sky;
feel its softness—
touch the blue;
all made by God
for me and you.

— Joan Stephen

Earth's Spirit shares with us
a feather, a pebble, or a whisper.

— Sara Sanderson

THE NEW KITTENS

The new kittens opened their eyes today!
I wonder, God,
Are they as amazed to see me
As I am to see them?

— Betty Williamson

Graces and
Blessings

MAY YOU ALWAYS BE BLESSED

May you always be blessed with
    a sky full of stars for your wishes
    a field of daisies at your front door
    the touch of a friend nearby.

May you always be blessed with
    a cloud as your pillow each night
    a kite with a string that goes on forever
    the fragrance of a summer rain.

May you always be blessed with
      a bouquet of leaves in the fall
      a rainbow leading to your dreams
      the music of a day ending.

May you always be blessed with
      a rocking chair to hold you in rest
      an angel in the snow
      the soft purr of a sleeping kitten.

Every day may you wake to smiles and hugs.
Every night may you dream of laughter and songs.

— Kathleen Haeny

ALL KINDS OF THANKS

For the food upon my plate,
I say "thank you very much."
For the clothes upon my back,
I say "merci beaucoup."
For the sandals on my feet,
I say "arigato."
For the books upon my desk,
I say "muchas gracias."
For the blessings of this day,
I give "thanks" in lots of ways.

— Martha K. Baker

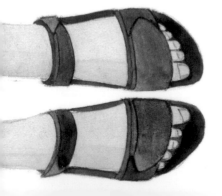

PRAYER FOR LITTLE CHILDREN

From head to foot
I am made in the image of God.
From my heart right into my hands
I feel the breath of God.
When I speak with my mouth
I follow the will of God.
When I behold God
In father and mother,
In all dear people,
In animal and flower,
In tree and stone,
Nothing can fill me with fear,
But only with love for all that is about me.

— Rudolf Steiner

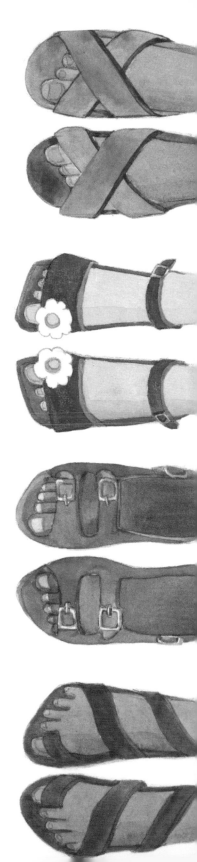

IN OUR HOME

We choose happiness
think good thoughts
have faith
say I'm sorry
listen and encourage
show respect
keep our promises
find the good
value family
forgive each other
use kind words
count our blessings
believe in love

— Lori Eberhardy

EYES

I thank you God for eyes that see,
a tiny bug, a tall, green tree,
soft pink clouds in summer sky,
wee hummingbirds that dip and fly,
the moon, bright stars, a satellite,
that moves above the earth tonight.

— Jane Porter Meier

DEAR GOD

I'm a creator,
writing a song,
playing my flute,
or strumming along.

Baking some bread,
or planting some seeds,
building a bridge,
or pulling the weeds.

Cleaning my room,
or washing the dishes,
reading a book,
or feeding the fishes.

I'm a creator,
whatever I do,
but where would I be
if I didn't have You?

— Risa Roberta Goldberg

BE THOU A BRIGHT FLAME

Be thou a bright flame before me,
be thou a guiding star above me,
be thou a smooth path below me,
be thou a kindly shepherd behind me,
today, tonight, and forever.

— From the *Carmina Gadelica*

BLESS THE PEOPLE

God of all our cities,
Each alley, street, and square,
Please look down on every house
And bless the people there.

— Joan Gale Thomas

I CAN BE KIND

I can be kind, although I am small.
I can be kind, to one, or to all.
I can be kind, in all sorts of ways.
I can be kind, when I go to play.
I can be kind in word and in deed.
I can be kind with thank you and please.
I can be kind, to people I know.
I can be kind, wherever I go.
I can be kind, as kind as can be.
I can be kind to you and to me!

— Leslie Paramore

HURT NO LIVING THING

Hurt no living thing;
Ladybird, nor butterfly,
Nor moth with dusty wing,
Nor cricket chirping cheerily,
Nor grasshopper so light of leap.
Nor dancing gnat, nor beetle fat,
Nor harmless worms that creep.

— Christina Rossetti

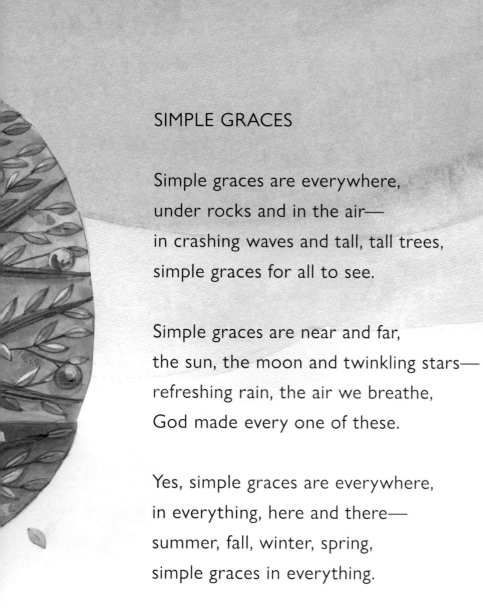

SIMPLE GRACES

Simple graces are everywhere,
under rocks and in the air—
in crashing waves and tall, tall trees,
simple graces for all to see.

Simple graces are near and far,
the sun, the moon and twinkling stars—
refreshing rain, the air we breathe,
God made every one of these.

Yes, simple graces are everywhere,
in everything, here and there—
summer, fall, winter, spring,
simple graces in everything.

— Jill Noblit MacGregor

THE POWER OF ONE

One candle can light a great dark room,
one smile can lift the saddest heart,
one word can give the hopeless hope,
and one person, taking a tiny part,
can change the world for good or bad,
but, oh, the power of good!
We need to believe in the power of one—
could it start with me? Yes, it could.

— Betty Williamson

Little deeds of kindness,
little words of love,
help to make earth happy,
like the heaven above.

— Julia Fletcher Carney

BE

Be brave like the lion,
gentle as sheep.
Be kind to all creatures
who swim, soar, or creep.
Be patient, tread lightly,
make friends on the way.
Be thankful and notice
each wonder-full day.

— Michelle Heidenrich Barnes

A CHILD'S PRAYER

God make my life a little light
Within the world to glow;
A little flame that burneth bright,
Wherever I may go.

— Matilda Barbara Betham-Edwards

Family and
Friends

WHEN I NEED A FRIEND

When I need a friend,

help me, first, to be a good one.

When a friend needs me,

help me, always, to care with courage.

When I am a friend,

help me, forever, to love with kindness.

— Martha K. Baker

ALL MY FRIENDS

Thank you, God,
for animal friends
and people friends,
for pretend friends
and school friends,
for family friends
and neighborhood friends,
and thank you, God, for me
because I'm a friend too!

— Barbara Younger

OUR FAMILY

Our family comes from many homes.
Our hair is straight. Our hair is brown.
Our hair is curled. Our eyes are blue.
Our skins are different colors, too.

We're girls and boys. We're big and small.
We're young and old. We're short and tall.
We're everything that we can be
and still we are a family.

— Author unknown

BLESS OUR FAMILY

Bless our family with peace and joy,
may our words to each other be kind
and our actions gentle.

— Anya Cara

HEARTS IN MY POCKET

Some days my home is here:
trains rattle past my room,
taxis honk below.
Daddy and I eat noodly soup
and watch the sun's rays sink
below the skyscrapers.

Some days my home is here:
maple trees in my front yard,
bicycle bells ring "Hello!"
Mommy and I color hearts
to share with our neighbors
when they pass by.

Always
I carry hearts
inside my pocket
and know God loves me
wherever I go.

— Nancy Tupper Ling

A PERFECT PAIR

My friend and I
are a perfect pair.
We go together
like honey and bear.
Like ball and bat
or naps and cat;
Like ocean and whale
or sand and pail;
Like ice cream and cone
or dog and bone;
Like snow and sled
or pillow and head;
My friend and I are
like hand and glove.
We're a perfect pair—
Like friendship and love.

— Claudia Kramer Kohlbrenner

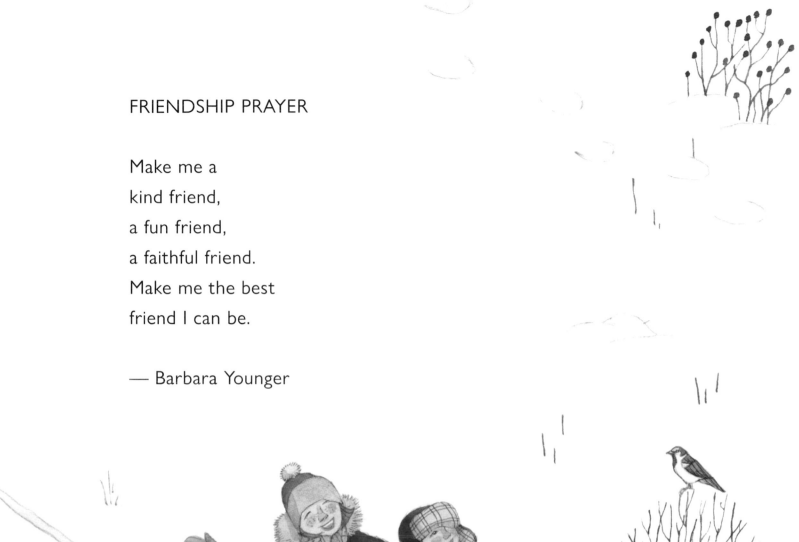

FRIENDSHIP PRAYER

Make me a
kind friend,
a fun friend,
a faithful friend.
Make me the best
friend I can be.

— Barbara Younger

PEACE

Peace be to this house
and all who dwell in it.
Peace be to them that enter
and to them that depart.

— Author unknown

THERE IS A LIGHT THAT SHINES

There is a light that shines
    beyond all things on earth,
    beyond us all,
    beyond the heavens,
    beyond the highest,
    the very highest heavens.
This is the light that shines in your heart.

— From the *Chandogya Upanishad*

I love God
and God loves me.
Here's to God
and family!

— Mary Lenore Quigley

CIRCLES

I see circles in passing—
those of prayer,
puddles of rain,
curls and noodles in baby hair.
I see circles of clouds,
circles of stars,
circles of love,
joining hearts of friends and family,
on earth and from above.

— Annie Dougherty

MY FAMILY'S HOME

If I could search the world around,
and joy within my heart be found
I know what I would love the best—
my family's home where I am blessed.

— Nancy Tupper Ling

Nightfall

THANKS TO THE SUN

Dear old Goldenface
we praise you
for your beaming light
for the smile of your early rises
for your laughter over the noon
for your goodnight grin
Be sure to come back tomorrow

— James Broughton

PRAISE

I praise the sun
that lifts my eyes.

I praise the day
that sunlight brings.

I praise the light
that lets me read.

I praise the dark
that brings me sleep.

I praise the stars
that burn so bright.

I praise the night
when angels sing.

I lift this song
to heaven's high.

I sing this song
to praise the light.

— Peter Markus

GIFTS FROM GOD

Before the end of every day
something good will come my way—
a hug, good deed, or smile for me
are gifts from God for ME to see!

— Mary C. Hancock

SHINE

Sunlight
Moonlight
Starlight
The light of God is with me
Everywhere
Always
Forever

— Carol Hort

IF YOU FEEL ALONE IN BED

If you get lonely in your bed,
then don't forget, dear sleepy head,
that while you lie there, all around
others, too, are lying down:

wolves with tails across their noses;
bees who dream of morning roses;
squirrels rocking high in trees;
camels settling to their knees;

baby whales beside their mothers
with the ocean waves for covers;
wombats, pandas, kinkajous,
each deliciously a-snooze;

birds with heads beneath their wings;
mother bat as baby clings;
rabbits in their winter burrows
dreaming slowly toward tomorrow . . .

If you feel lonely in your bed,
then don't forget, my sleepy head:
all night long, as darkness lulls,
you're sleeping with the Animals.

— Tim Myers

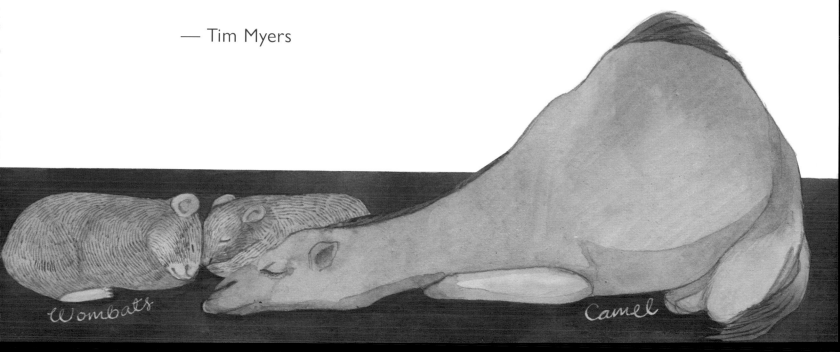

LULLABY

Slowly, slowly, slowly now
by the fading of the light
the day finds calm and comfort
in the silence of the night.

Softly, softly, softly now
like whispers filled with love
the playful sounds of day are hushed
by the peace of stars above.

Sweetly, sweetly, sweetly now
have dreams of rainbow hue
oh, sleep well, my lovely one
God's blanket covers you.

Slowly, softly, sweetly now
God's blanket covers you.

— Daniel Roselle

A NIGHTTIME PRAYER

Dear God, I thank you for the night
that gives us time to rest,
I thank you, too, for our safe home
and those I love the best.

— Jane Porter Meier

INTO GOD'S GOOD NIGHT

My toys are still. My books are closed.
My grown-ups say good night.

My bed is warm, my pillow soft.
My blankets close me 'round.

Your day was bright. Your night is here.
You fill it with your love.

Thank you, God, for all these things.
Thank you, God, for you.

— Barbara Falconer Newhall

DAY'S END

Night is come,
Owls are out;
Beetles hum
Round about.

Children snore
Safe in bed;
Nothing more
Need be said.

— Henry Newbolt

FROM THE NAVAJO NIGHT WAY SONG

May it be delightful my house;
From my head may it be delightful;
To my feet may it be delightful;
Where I lie may it be delightful;
All above me may it be delightful;
All around me may it be delightful.

— Author unknown

GOOD-NIGHT POEM

Now the long day
feels complete.

Tuck your feet
between clean sheets.

Tuck your body
into bed.

Tuck sweet dreams
into your head.

Tuck your covers
snug and tight.

Tuck the good
into the night.

— Ralph Fletcher

LITTLE SURPRISES

Today has been a busy day,
Books to read and games to play.
God bless my friends and family,
The ones who love and care for me.
Thank you for the world to see.
Thank you God for all that's me.
Time to sleep and close my eyes.
Tomorrow is a new surprise.

— Susan Paurazas

Dreams

SEA OF DREAMS

Sleepy time travels wait for me
as I set out on dreamland's sea.
Waves of slumber and welcome rest
invite me on a night-time quest.

As dreams roll by, I catch a ride
with dolphins swimming by my side.
They welcome us to join their play
at water's edge that sunny day.

We laugh and build sandcastles high
while seagulls spread their wings to fly.
Then sunlight fades my ocean dream,
I realize things aren't as they seem.

Waves of dreams that build and billow
return me to my comfy pillow.
And though I've traveled wide and deep,
I did it while I was asleep.

— Susanne Wiggins Bunch

GOOD NIGHT, MOONLIGHT!

Good night,
moonlight.
Good night,
star bright.
Good night,
moonbeams.
Good night,
cricket wings.

Good night,
moonlight.
Good night,
sleep tight.
Good night,
sweet dreams.
Good night,
everything!

— Jill Noblit MacGregor

GREAT OWL OF DREAMS

Great Owl of Dreams,
Wings soft and furred with dark,
Soar through my sleep
To that tender place between
The eyes and heart.
Bring me the dream in your mother beak,
The dream to feed me and teach me
And guide me,
Great Owl of Dreams.

— Cait Johnson

TONIGHT . . .

I will dream
of the blue pigeon
who spread her feathers
and cooed for me at the zoo

and the purple morning glories—
the ones that made
Mama smile today,
they'll dance overhead.

And I will say:
Mama, their blossoms
looked like fingers
waving to the people.

And in my perfect dream
an orange fox will sit beside me
far beneath a golden gate
until the fog rolls in.

— Nancy Tupper Ling

DREAMS ALLOWED

Don't be afraid to dream aloud
the things you want to do;
just saying what is in your heart
will help your dreams come true.

— Charles Ghigna

DREAMS

Thunderstorms and dogs with wings,
lots of silly no-name things,
blowing bubbles in the breeze,
feeding lions nuts and cheese,
roads that don't go anywhere,
purple trees, a hungry bear—
sometimes, when my dreams are bad,
I wake up feeling scared or sad.
"Thank you, God," I always say,
"For making bad dreams go away."

— Mary Ryer

WHAT DO YOU DREAM?

Teddy bear, teddy bear,
What do you dream?

I dream of the salmon
That splash in the stream,
And fairy-tale forests
With towering trees,
And blueberry bushes
And honey from bees.
When you go to sleep
Do you dream like I do?

I dream of these poems
I'm reading with you.

— Kenn Nesbitt

STAR LIGHT, STAR BRIGHT

Star light, star bright,
may all your dreams come true.
Good night, sleep tight,
and may God watch over you.

Something to drink—a story to read,
a "lay me down to sleep."
A special wish—a good night kiss,
"I pray the Lord to keep."

A hug good night, so you'll sleep tight,
now close those sleepy eyes
and fly away to dreamland
on a magic carpet ride.

— Mary Lenore Quigley

SOMEWHERE

Would you tell me the way to Somewhere?
    Somewhere, *Some*where,
    I have heard of a place called Somewhere —
    But know not where it can be.
        It makes no difference,
        Whether or not
        I go in dreams
        Or trudge on foot:
Could you tell me the way to Somewhere,
    The Somewhere meant for me.

— Walter de la Mare

THE DREAMLAND TRAIN

There's one little train to Dreamland—
All aboard!

One little engine puffing magic steam—
All aboard!

One little engineer with eyes agleam—
All aboard!

One little station, tickets free inside—
All aboard!

One little yawn—that's all it costs to ride—
All aboard!

One little eye to close, and then the other—
All aboard!

And then a million wonders to discover!
All aboard!

— Tim Myers

PERMISSIONS AND ACKNOWLEDGMENTS

Grateful acknowledgment is made to the authors and publishers for the use of the following material.
Every effort has been made to contact original sources.
If notified, the publishers will be pleased to rectify an omission in future editions.
Please visit the authors' websites to view and purchase their books.

Martha K. Baker for "All Kinds of Thanks" and "When I Need a Friend."
Michelle Heidenrich Barnes for "Be." www.MichelleHBarnes.com
Patricia Spears Bigelow for "Rejoicing."
Susanne Wiggins Bunch for "My Day Begins with Kisses," "Sea of Dreams," and "Sky Dancers."
Anya Cara for "Bless Our Family."
Jane Mary Curran for "The Beach."
Barb Dodge for "Earth's Spirit Shares with Us" by Sara Sanderson.
Annie Dougherty for "Circles" and "Morning."
Lori Eberhardy for "In Our Home."
Susan J. Erickson for "Waking Up Prayer." www.susanjerickson.com
Ralph Fletcher for "Good-Night Poem." www.ralphfletcher.com
Charles Ghigna for "Dreams Allowed." www.FatherGoose.com
Risa Roberta Goldberg for "Dear God." www.simplymarvelousorganizing.com
Kathleen Haeny for "May You Always Be Blessed."
Cait Johnson for "Great Owl of Dreams." Published in *Celebrating the Great Mother: A Handbook of Earth-Honoring Activities for Parents and Children.* © 1995 by Cait Johnson and Maura D. Shaw. Published by Inner Traditions. www.caitjohnson.com
Jan Jolowski for "Sometimes" by Joan Stephen.
Sherry Jungwirth for "My Beautiful Day," "The Butterfly Ballet," and "You're Everywhere" by Marion Schoeberlein.
Claudia Kramer Kohlbrenner for "A Perfect Pair."
Fanny M. Levin for "Wherever I Am."
Arlene Gay Levine for "Creation." www.arlenegaylevine.com
Nancy Tupper Ling for "For Every Little Thing," "Hearts in My Pocket," "My Family's Home," and "Tonight." www.nancytupperling.com www.finelinepoets.com
The Literary Trustees of Walter de la Mare and the Society of Authors as their Representative for "Somewhere" by Walter de la Mare.
Jill Noblit MacGregor for "Good Night, Moonlight!" and "Simple Graces."
Peter Markus for "Praise." www.dzancbooks.org/our-books/inside-my-pencil-teaching-poetry-in-detroit-public-schools
Tim Myers for "The Dreamland Train" and "If You Feel Alone in Bed." https://www.scu.edu/english/faculty-staff/tim-myers
Kenn Nesbitt for "What Do You Dream?" www.poetry4kids.com
Barbara Falconer Newhall for "Into God's Good Night." www.BarbaraFalconerNewhall.com
Lynn Olson for "Lullaby" and "The Wonderer" by Daniel Roselle.
Leslie Paramore for "I Can Be Kind." www.sparklerprincess.com
Susan Paurazas for "Little Surprises."
Mary Lenore Quigley for "I Love God" and "Star Light, Star Bright." www.Q2lnk.com
Mary Ryer for "Dreams."
Rabbi Rami M. Shapiro for "Seeing You." www.rabbirami.com
Joel Singer for "Thanks to the Sun" by James Broughton.
Nicole VanderMeer for "Bugs."
Betty Williamson for "The New Kittens" and "The Power of One."
Barbara Younger for "All My Friends" and "Friendship Prayer." https://barbarakyounger.com/art

INDEX